PRACTICE MAKES PERFECT

★ ★ ★ ★

ISBN- 978-0-9963948-3-3

First Edition

Published in the United States

Entered in the Library of Congress

Table of Contents

Vocabulary

Week 1

Word	Definition
Abet (v)	To help, encourage, or support someone in a criminal act
Component (n)	One of the parts of something (such as a system or mixture); an important piece of something
Pithy (adj)	Using few words in a clever and effective way
Eccentric (adj)	Tending to act in strange or unusual ways
Fallacy (n)	A wrong belief: a false or mistaken idea
Plausible (adj)	Possibly true: believable or realistic
Irascible (adj)	Becoming angry very easily: having a bad temper
Assail (v)	To attack or criticize (someone or something) in a violent or angry way
Fastidious (adj)	Very careful about how you do something
Onslaught (adj)	A violent attack
Intricate (adj)	Having many parts
Turbulent (adj)	Moving in an irregular or violent way
Exotic (adj)	Very different, strange, or unusual
Culminate (v)	To reach the end or the final result of something
Pungent (adj)	Having a strong, sharp taste or smell
Grapple (v)	To try to solve a problem; to hold and fight with another person
Audacious (adj)	Very confident and daring; very bold and surprising or shocking
Susceptible (adj)	Easily affected, influenced, or harmed by something
Deploy (v)	To organize and send out (people or things) to be used for a particular purpose
Enigma (n)	Someone or something that is difficult to understand or explain

Week 2

Word	Definition
Ornate (adj)	Covered with decorations
Porous (adj)	Easy to pass or get through
Decipher (v)	To uncover
Agile (adj)	Someone or something that can move quickly and in different directions
Lucrative (adj)	Producing money or wealth
Augment (v)	To increase the size or amount of something
Desolate (adj)	To make someone feel very sad and lonely
Atrocity (n)	A very cruel or terrible act or action
Aloof (adj)	Not involved with or friendly toward other people
Renounce (v)	To say especially in a formal or official way that you will no longer have or accept (something); to formally give up (something)
Recourse (n)	An opportunity or choice to use or do something in order to deal with a problem or situation
Vilify (v)	To say or write very harsh and critical things about (someone or something)
Fortify (v)	To make something or someone stronger
Serene (adj)	Calm and peaceful
Formidable (adj)	Very powerful or strong
Excruciating (adj)	Very painful
Gaunt (adj)	Very thin, usually because of illness or suffering
Disgruntled (adj)	Upset or frustrated
Imperative (adj)	Very important
Languish (v)	To continue for a long time without activity or progress in an unpleasant or unwanted situation

Week 3

Word	Definition
Connoisseur (n)	a person who knows a lot about something (such as art, wine, food, etc.) : an expert in a particular subject
Encroach (v)	to gradually move or go into an area that is beyond the usual or desired limits
Tedious (adj)	Time-consuming
Benign (adj)	Not causing death or serious injury
Convey (v)	To take or carry something or someone from one place to another
Deplore (v)	To hate or dislike something
Inaugurate (v)	To introduce (someone, such as a newly elected official) into a job or position with a formal ceremony
Muster (v)	To work hard to find or get something (like courage or support)
Sporadic (adj)	Every now and then
Flustered (v)	To be embarrassed; caught off guard
Trepidation (n)	Fear
Crusade (n)	To take part in a major effort to change something
Gingerly (adv)	Very carefully
Preposterous (adj)	Ridiculous or absurd
Succumb (v)	To give in
Conscientious (adj)	Considerate
Dire (adj)	In much need
Defect (n)	A problem or fault that makes someone or something not perfect
Voracious (adj)	Having or showing a tendency to eat very large amounts of food
Swelter (adj)	To be very hot and uncomfortable

Week 4

Word	Definition
Adept (adj)	Very good at doing something that is not easy
Liberal (adj)	Not opposed to new ideas or ways of behaving that are not traditional or widely accepted
Proficient (adj)	Good at doing something
Deceptive (adj)	Intended to make someone believe something that is not true
Revenue (n)	Money that is made by or paid to a business or an organization
Capacious (adj)	Able to hold or contain a lot: large in capacity
Exemplify (v)	To be a very good example of (something): to show (something) very clearly
Chastise (v)	To criticize (someone) harshly for doing something wrong
Hindrance (n)	A person or thing that makes a situation difficult: a person or thing that hinders someone or something
Decree (n)	An official order given by a person with power or by a government
Incense (v)	To make (someone) very angry
Apprehend (v)	To notice and understand (something)
Strident (adj)	Sounding harsh and unpleasant
Modify (v)	To alter or fix
Reception (n)	A social gathering to celebrate something or to welcome someone
Commemorate (v)	To remember someone or something
Conservative (adj)	Not liking or accepting changes or new ideas
Vie (v)	To compete with others in an attempt to get or win something
Assimilate (v)	To take in information, ideas, or culture and understand it fully
Shackle (v)	To prevent people from acting freely

Week 5

Word	Definition
Pivotal (adj)	A very important change
Surpass (v)	To be better or greater than (someone or something)
Disdain (adj)	A feeling of strong dislike or disapproval of someone or something you think does not deserve respect
Rational (adj)	Based on facts or reason and not on emotions or feelings
Gullible (adj)	Easily fooled or cheated
Servile (adj)	Very obedient and trying too hard to please someone
Tirade (n)	A long and angry speech
Foster (v)	To help (something) grow or develop
Subside (v)	To become less strong or intense
Haven (n)	A place where you are protected from danger and trouble
Wrangle (v)	To argue angrily with someone
Awry (adj)	Not working correctly or happening in the expected way
Discern (v)	To see, hear, or notice something with difficulty or effort
Overt (adj)	Easily seen; not secret or hidden
Deter (v)	To cause someone to decide not to do something
Ungainly (adv)	Moving in an awkward or clumsy way; not graceful
Foreboding (n)	A feeling that something bad is going to happen
Doctrine (n)	A set of ideas or beliefs that are taught or believed to be true
Luminous (adj)	Producing or seeming to produce light

Vocabulary Quizzes

Week 1

For questions 1 -2, write the definition for the following words.

1. Assail

    _____

    _____

2. Eccentric

    _____

    _____

For questions 3 – 6, choose the word that matches the definition.

3. A violent attack
    a. susceptible
    b. onslaught
    c. fallacy
    d. intricate

4. Moving in an irregular or violent way
    a. irascible
    b. pungent
    c. turbulent
    d. deploy

5. Someone or something that is difficult to understand or explain
    a. plausible
    b. enigma
    c. fallacy
    d. abet

6. To reach the end or final result of something
    a. pithy
    b. onslaught
    c. exotic
    d. culminate

For questions 7 – 8, use the vocab word in a sentence that demonstrates its meaning.

7. Audacious

_____

_____

8. Grapple

_____

_____

For questions 9 – 10, choose the word from the word bank that best matches the context of the sentence.

Abet	Turbulent	Susceptible	Fallacy	Pungent	Deploy

9. Jorge was _____ to hives if he ate strawberries. He hated being allergic!

10. I can't handle chopping onions! They have such a_____ smell.

Week 2

For questions 1 -2, write the definition for the following words.

1. Ornate

_____

_____

2. Disgruntled

_____

_____

For questions 3 – 6, choose the word that matches the definition.

3. Not involved with or friendly toward other people
    a. porous
    b. desolate
    c. disgruntled
    d. aloof

4. Very thin, usually because of illness or suffering
    a. languish
    b. gaunt
    c. agile
    d. recourse

5. Very painful
    a. augment
    b. excruciating
    c. imperative
    d. vilify

6. Calm and peaceful
    a. serene
    b. atrocity
    c. ornate
    d. augment

For questions 7 – 8, use the vocab word in a sentence that demonstrates its meaning.

7. Lucrative

_____

_____

8. Fortify

_____

_____

For questions 9 – 10, choose the word from the word bank that best matches the context of the sentence.

Formidable	Desolate	Imperative	Agile	Aloof

9. It is _____that you bring a warm jacket to any east coast college town. It's cold walking to class from December-February!

10. In football, you have to be _____, or you will get tackled early!

Week 3

For questions 1 -2, write the definition for the following words.

1. Preposterous

_____

_____

2. Voracious

_____

_____

For questions 3 – 6, choose the word that matches the definition.

3. To take or carry something or someone from one place to another
    a. encroach
    b. dire
    c. covey
    d. succumb

4. Very carefully
    a. muster
    b. gingerly
    c. defect
    d. trepidation

5. To be embarrassed; caught off guard
    a. flustered
    b. conscientious
    c. tedious
    d. crusade

6. A problem or fault that makes someone or something not perfect
   a. benign
   b. inaugurate
   c. trepidation
   d. defect

For questions 7 – 8, use the vocab word in a sentence that demonstrates its meaning.

7. Gingerly

_____

_____

8. Swelter

_____

_____

For questions 9 – 10, choose the word from the word bank that best matches the context of the sentence.

Deplore	Sporadic	Muster	Connoisseur	Tedious

9. I _____ when people leave the cap off the toothpaste!

10. I've always wanted to try skydiving…now I just need to _____ up the courage.

Week 4

For questions 1 -2, write the definition for the following words.

1. Decree

_____

_____

2. Modify

_____

_____

For questions 3 – 6, choose the word that matches the definition.

3. Not opposed to new ideas or ways of behaving that are not traditional
    a. conservative
    b. liberal
    c. strident
    d. commemorate

4. To take in information, ideas, or culture, and understand it fully
    a. proficient
    b. apprehend
    c. vie
    d. assimilate

5. To make someone very angry
    a. adept
    b. revenue
    c. Incense
    d. exemplify

6. A social gathering to celebrate something or to welcome
   a. commemorate
   b. reception
   c. revenue
   d. hindrance

For questions 7 – 8, use the vocab word in a sentence that demonstrates its meaning.

7. Apprehend

   _____

   _____

8. Proficient

   _____

   _____

For questions 9 – 10, choose the word from the word bank that best matches the context of the sentence.

Hindrance	Vie	Capacious	Deceptive	Chastises

9. My mom always _____ me for eating her cookies before we eat dinner.

10. The D- on my report card is a _____ as I am applying top colleges.

Week 5

For questions 1 -2, write the definition for the following words.

1. Haven

_____

_____

2. Tirade

_____

_____

For questions 3 – 6, choose the word that matches the definition.

3. A very important change
    a. pivotal
    b. gullible
    c. overt
    d. deter

4. Not working correctly or happening in an expected way
    a. foreboding
    b. doctrine
    c. awry
    d. disdain

5. Based on facts or reason and not on emotions or feelings
    a. discern
    b. ungainly
    c. subside
    d. rational

6. To cause someone to decide not to do something
    a. deter
    b. foster
    c. luminous
    d. distain

For questions 7 – 8, use the vocab word in a sentence that demonstrates its meaning.

7. Foster

_____

_____

8. Ungainly

_____

_____

For questions 9 – 10, choose the word from the word bank that best matches the context of the sentence.

Gullible	Overt	Subside	Doctrine	Ungainly	Foreboding

9. Jenny was _____ the first time she tried on high heels, stumbling and falling three times in 5 blocks.

10. Martin's headache began to _____ after taking Tylenol and putting a cold washcloth over his head.

Passion Mapping Activity

Brainstorm

1. What do you currently like or love? What are your favorite classes? (Examples: soccer, music, shopping, hanging with friends etc.). Please come up with 5-10 examples.

2. How do you like to spend your time when you're not in school? (Example: Describe your perfect day.)

3. If you could read/learn about anything in the world, what would it be? What do you wonder about? (Example: Is there life on other planets? How do you become a Billboard Top 100 artist?)

4. After discussing your answers to questions 1-3, use your fellow mentors and teacher to create three professions that align to your passions. (Example: Love writing→ journalist, love to play sports→ Soccer Team Manager, love music→ Music producer)

Create the Passion Map

Occupation: _____

Field: (Circle)

Architecture and City Planning	Arts and Entertainment	Business	Communications
Engineering and Computer Science	Environment	Government	Health and Medicine
Nonprofit and Social Justice	Sciences- Biological and Physical	Law and Public Policy	Education

Other: _____

Road to Your Career: Using another piece of paper, create a road map that will prepare you for your chosen career. This can involve the type of college you need to go to, your major, classes, internships, professional tests, companies etc. Please note, you may have to do research to complete this activity.

Example: Job: Teacher in New York City

1. Apply to Hunter College 2. Major in Adolescent Education 3. Complete internships at organizations like Breakthrough, Practice Makes Perfect, BELL, and summer camps 4. Student-teach for two semesters 5. Take the LAST, ATS-W, and a content specialty test 5. Enroll in Master's program at Fordham University in Adolescent Education 6. Receive New York State teacher license in Adolescent Social Studies Education 7-12. 7. Teach full-time!

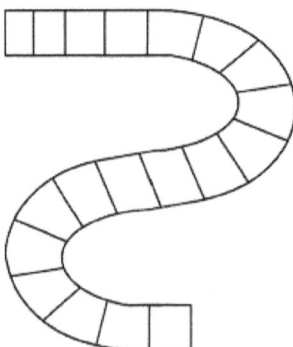

Writing Component

Directions: Using the roadmap you created, write about your new career and what it will take to get there. Make sure to explain all the components you used in your road map.

Writing Workshop

Day 1: Pick an Expository Prompt and Brainstorm

Directions: Mentors will craft an expository writing piece that includes an introduction, opinion statement, 3 pieces of evidence, and a concluding paragraph. To successfully write an expository piece, mentors will complete a brainstorming sheet, a graphic organizer, a first draft, and a final draft. Teaching Fellows will grade assignment and provide mentor with a rubric.

Prompt Selection—please select a prompt from the list below:

Teachers have a way of changing our lives and/or helping us achieve what we never thought was possible. Describe the most effective teacher you have ever had and how she impacted your life.
Normally, people choose their friends because of commonalities. But this is not always the case. Explain how two people of different interests and backgrounds could become unlikely allies. Support your ideas with examples and details.
Everyone has one item that is important to him or her. Think about one item that is important to you and why. It could be something you found, made, or had given to you. Write an essay explaining why this one item is important to you. Support your ideas with examples and details.
Age has a funny way of making changes. It is probably easy for you to look back and see that you and your friends have made some major changes since you left the elementary grades. Your teachers and friends may be different, your school may be different, and some of your interests are probably different. Think back to fourth grade and describe how school has changed for you as a seventh grader. Support your ideas with examples and details.
All of us face challenges in life. One challenge might be making friends. Another challenge might be learning how to play a sport or musical instrument. Describe a challenge that you or someone you know has faced. What lessons did you learn? Support your ideas with examples and details.
A famous businessman once said, "Players win games; teams win championships." Think carefully about the following statement. Sometimes you can accomplish good things by yourself but better things with other people. Explain whether it is better to work by yourself or with a group.

Brainstorm

Directions: Using the space below, brainstorm some ideas for the prompt you selected. What are some examples you will use? What are some phrases, words, facts, figures you want to make sure to include?

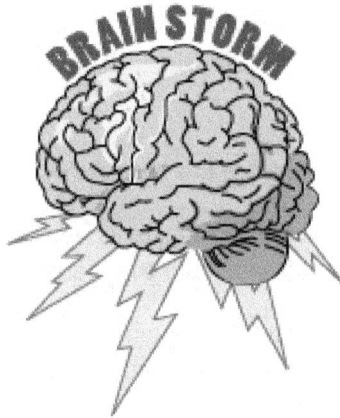

Day 2: Using a Graphic Organizer

Paragraph 1: Introduction	
Topic Sentence	
Description or Background on issue or topic	
Closing sentence/thesis	

Paragraph 2	Paragraph 3	Paragraph 4
Evidence 1:	Evidence 2:	Evidence 3:
Details and Examples	Details and Examples	Details and Examples

Conclusion	
Restate thesis (hint reread intro)	
Summarize 3 pieces of evidence	
Closing statement	

Day 3: First Draft

Rubric: Mentors will be graded on a rubric that will help them see where they excelled and where they can improve.

	Professional	Semi-Professional	Still in the Minor Leagues	Working to Get on the Team
Focus/ Opinion (20)	--Responds skillfully to all parts of the prompt --States an opinion that demonstrates an insightful understanding of topic	--Responds to all parts of the prompt --States an opinion that demonstrates an understanding of the topic	--Responds to most parts of the prompt --States an opinion that demonstrates limited understanding of topic	--Responds to some or no parts of the prompt --Does not state an opinion and/or demonstrates little to no understanding of topic
Organization (32)	--Organizes ideas and information into purposeful, coherent paragraphs that include an elaborated introduction with clear thesis, structured body, and insightful conclusion --Uses linking words, phrases, and clauses skillfully to connect reasons to opinion	--Organizes ideas and information into logical introductory, body, and concluding paragraphs --Uses linking words and phrases appropriately to connect reasons to opinion	--Organizes ideas and information in an attempted paragraph structure that includes a sense of introduction, body and conclusion --Uses some linking words and/or phrases to connect reasons to opinion but simplistically	--Does not organize ideas and information coherently due to lack of paragraph structure and/or a missing introduction, body, or conclusion --Uses no linking words or phrases
Support/ Evidence (40)	--Supports opinion skillfully with substantial and relevant facts, details, and/or reasons --Provides insightful explanation/analysis of how evidence supports opinion	--Supports opinion with relevant facts, details, and/or reasons --Provides clear explanation/ analysis of how evidence supports opinion	--Supports opinion with minimal and/or irrelevant facts, details, and/or reasons --Provides some explanation/ analysis of how evidence supports opinion	--Does not support opinion with facts, details, and/or reasons --Provides no or inaccurate explanation/analysis of how evidence supports opinion
Language/ Word Choice /Grammar/ Mechanics/ Spelling (8)	--Uses purposeful, correct, and varied sentence structures --Demonstrates creativity and flexibility when using conventions (grammar, punctuation, capitalization, and spelling) to enhance meaning --Uses half of the prescribed vocabulary words	--Uses correct and varied sentence structures --Demonstrates grade level appropriate conventions; errors are minor and do not obscure meaning --Uses a fourth of the prescribed vocabulary words	--Uses some repetitive yet correct sentence structure --Demonstrates some grade level appropriate conventions, but errors obscure meaning --Uses less than a fourth of the prescribed vocabulary words	--Does not demonstrate sentence mastery --Demonstrates limited understanding of grade level appropriate conventions, and errors interfere with the meaning --Uses no academic or domain-specific vocabulary
Total				
Comments				

Tic-Tac-Toe Book Assignment

Directions: Using the book you have read, complete a "tic tac toe" worth of assignments. After your 3 assignments are done, you will present one of the assignments to your classmates. Activities should have rough drafts on the pages provides and final drafts on printer paper or lined loose-leaf paper.

Write a letter to the main character in your book and the character's reply. Use at least 10 of your vocabulary words in the assignment.	Describe three characters from the story. List reasons why you would or wouldn't be friends with these people.	Write a script and act out a scene from the book and present it to your classmates.
Create a book jacket, including illustrations, an enticing summary, and two favorable reviews.	Write a poem or song about the characters and events in your story. Set the words to music of a popular song and sing it to the class.	Explain why you think this book will or will not be read 100 years from now. Support your opinion using 10 of your vocabulary words and stating 3 specific events in the story.
Prepare a television commercial about your book. Act out the commercial for your classmates.	Write a different ending to your book. Use 10 of your vocabulary words in your response.	Write a letter or email to a close friend recommending the book you have just read.

Activity 1

Activity: _____

Activity 2

Activity: _____

Activity 3

Activity: _____

Successful High School Experiences

Twelve High School Myths

Directions: Read the following statements and mark whether you believe they are true (T) or false (F).

Statement	True or False
1. Every Friday, freshman are hazed or bullied by upperclassmen.	
2. Your high school years are best years of your life.	
3. Appearance is the key to success.	
4. You'll be friends with your high school friends for the rest of your life	
5. Food fights are amazing and happen at least once a month.	
6. You'll attend a house party every weekend.	
7. Popularity is everything in high school.	
8. There is designated seating in the cafeteria.	
9. The workload is unbearable. You will pull an "all nighter" every month.	
10. Junior year is the most challenging year of high school.	
11. Senior year will be a breeze.	
12. Colleges don't look at your senior year grades.	

What's a Myth and What is True

1. Freshmen Fridays do not exist. If you are being bullied by upperclassmen, tell an adult at your school. Freshmen have just as many rights as any other student at the school.

2. High school is just four years of your life. While movies and television put a lot of pressure on student to think that high school is the "end all be all," this is far from the truth. Those who work hard during high school (and forgo some of the parties) will have greater access to elite colleges. At college you can create a flexible school schedule with additional opportunities to explore and create your own academic and professional paths. Enjoy all eight years of fun, but remember that your decisions will affect your future.

3. Sadly, this is true for the rest of your life. Studies show that there is a correlation between success and beauty. For instance, a *Forbes* article found a study that said "NFL quarterbacks with good-looking facial features earned almost 12% more than their less attractive but equally skilled colleagues." Perception matters, so wear the right clothes (for example, to an interview or the first day of class) to make a good impression, and never forget to work diligently.

4. The veracity of this myth varies. It is unlikely that you will attend the same university as all your friends. The mere distance is enough to terminate some of those friendships, but if the distance does not, you and your friends are likely to change. How you deal with those changes will determine whether your friendship continues. Do not stress. If you want to maintain the friendship you can. If not, no big deal. You will develop new friendships in college.

5. As exciting as food fights appear on television, they are exceptionally rare and dreadful. No one wants to walk around school with ketchup in his hair and remnants of half eaten burgers in his collar. Unless you start a food fight yourself, you probably won't experience one, and I doubt you really want to experience one.

6. You will not attend a party every weekend while in high school. You and your friends may have parties, but not that frequently. Expect the occasional party or concert, but many more slow Friday and Saturday nights watching shows or facetiming with your friends.

7. Some people are, in fact, more popular than others, but it doesn't matter. Whether or not you are a member of the popular group, you will establish a group of friends who

share your interests and with whom you have a great time. At the end, real friendships matter more than popularity.

8. Seating in high school and even in college is a strange phenomenon. Regimented cafeteria seating is real, but develops organically. Chances are you will sit with your friends and together slowly decide on a seating location. It is subconscious like choosing a seat in the theater. The seat yours for the duration of the movie even if you leave it to use the restroom or purchase snacks. No one will oust you from your seat if you change locations, but you may feel uncomfortable when a group of people you do not know or with whom you are not good friends sits next to you and carries on a conversation without including you. Someone may even give you the evil eye.

9. Thankfully, this myth is false. The change in workload will require some acclimation period, and during this period, you may feel overloaded. Yet, like those before you, you will acclimate rather quickly. Please do not resort to extreme measure to cope with stress or an unusually heavy workload. Just manage your time appropriately, mediate, and exercise.

10. Every student will have a particular year that they find uniquely challenging. Junior year you begin your college search, you prepare for and take college entrance exams (SAT, SAT II, ACT), and you study for 2-4 Advanced Placement exams in addition regular high school curriculum and extracurricular activities. With thousands of universities to choose from, the college search alone is daunting. Luckily for you, you are starting this process early.

11. During your senior year you have to perfect your documents (personal statement, resume, etc.) and apply to colleges. If the application process does not stress you, the waiting most surely will. Senior year is often the most stressful year because you are applying to colleges, financial aid, and outside scholarships while maintaining a full course load filled with Advanced Placement classes. It can be a very stressful time, and as such, it is a great time to start exercising. Studies show that exercise reduces stress.

12. This is a bald-faced lie! Depending on the application deadline, colleges receive your first semester grades with your application. The university you choose to attend will request your final transcript, which includes your performance all four years of high school. Some schools may rescind their offer after receiving students' final transcripts. Do not slack off senior year.

Activity: Did any of the myths or truths surprise you? Pick one and in 3-4 sentences described why you were surprised.

Habits of a Successful Student

1. **Practice efficient time management and organization**
   Good time management and organizational skills are reciprocal. Managing one's time appropriately requires one to be organized. Organizing your activities requires good time management skills. You can begin doing both by not postponing small tasks. Why not? When small tasks accumulate, they aggregate into 20 10-minute jobs that require over 3 hours to complete. That's a waste of time.

2. **Manage your time effectively**
   - Get a planner, and use it to schedule your activities, study time, free time, and breaks.
   - Prioritize your activities by importance, time required, and due date.
   - Do not turn a 30-minute break turn into a 2-hour break.
   - You are less efficient when you multitask, so don't multitask.
   - Hold yourself accountable. If you planned to complete five tasks on Wednesday, complete those tasks on Wednesday. All incomplete tasks will rollover to the next day, thereby increasing your activity load and distorting your schedule for that day.

3. **Set attainable goals**
   Reach for the moon, but make sure you are planning accordingly. You can reach for the moon, but without means of transportation, you won't get there. This advice is about honesty, not dumbing down your dreams. Be honest about what you can achieve in the allotted time. If you truly desire something, dedicate the time and effort necessary to achieve it. If not, reevaluate.

4. **Study**
   The goal of education is not to generate students who regurgitate information, but rather to cultivate a group of critical thinkers. When studying, you should always focus on learning, not memorizing. To do so, review your notes daily, so you do not require hours or days before an exam to study; create study groups to correct misunderstandings and share knowledge; and concentrate on concepts (big picture). Then fill in the details.

5. **Take good notes**
   - Record the main idea, supplementary ideas, and important supporting details regardless of the format in which the information is presented
   - Look for connections between ideas.
   - Frequently ask yourself: "Will I understand what I am writing later? Can I explain this to someone not in class?" If not, then your notes are unclear.
   - Ask questions. From now on, "I did not know" is never an acceptable excuse. If you are unsure – or if you're just curious – ask immediately! This applies to school, work, and everything else.

6. **Complete all assignments**
Assignments are designed to help you practice, so you can solidify the information. Not turning in an assignment can hurt your grades and also hurt your relationship with your teachers.

7. **Take personal responsibility/ commitment**
Make a commitment to yourself to always behave in a manner that yields success, and to hold yourself accountable. If you plan to study for three hours, then study for three hours. Do not allow ephemeral indolence to hinder your success.

8. **Do some independent reading**
Reading improves your cognitive function, your comprehension of the structure of arguments, your ability to reason, and your grammar and vocabulary which all enhance your academic, professional, an civic functioning. Studies show that those who forgo reading miss as much information as those who cannot read, and that those who read voluntarily are better thinkers and are more successful than those who do not. The more you read, the better you will be at accurately processing information.

9. **Get some sleep**
Resist the pressure to prove diligence through lack of sleep, for it sleep is crucial for healthy brain function, emotional well-being, safety, and physical health. For more information on the importance of sleep read the following article, http://www.nhlbi.nih.gov/health/health-topics/topics/sdd/why.html

10. **Create a support system**
Choose your confidants carefully, and then trust them to support you. Share your frustrations with friends, family, teachers, coaches, mentors, and anyone else who supports you. Chances are they know more than you do, and if they do not, they can help you search for answers. Remember your Practice Makes Perfect family is always here for you.

11. **Have fun!**
High school is fun, so enjoy it! Join teams, organizations, and clubs within and outside of your high school and comfort zone. Participating in group activities is a great way to meet new people and expand your worldview.

Habits of A Successful Student

Directions: Choose 4 of the 11 habits of a successful student that you do not currently use and explain how you will implement them into your next school year.

Habit	How Will You Implement this Skill into the Next School Year?

Planning Your Schedule

Directions: Use the following syllabi and calendar to plan two weeks worth of activities on the calendar on the next page.

Week 6

Exam 1 on Topics 1-10: Wednesday, October 11

     Part II. Building the First Europe, C.E. 950 - 1200
     Topic 9   "The First Europe's Jewish Heritage"
     Topic 10   "Peasant Life and the Agricultural Revolution"

Thursday Discussion: None this week; exam instead!

Homework for Week 7 (Due Monday, October 16):
• The Medieval Record: Pp. 199 - 200 + ch. 8, "The Secular Orders of Society"
• Write a mini-essay on one of the "Mini-Essay Topics" for ch. 8 of The Medieval Record

---

Research Methods for Fall 2014 Schedule (continued)

Dates	Topic	Readings
Week 6		
Oct. 10	Experimental Design continued	Chapter 9
Oct. 12	Quiz 5	
Week 7		
Oct. 17	Methods Writing Due	
Oct. 19	Examination II (Ch. 5 - 9)	

October

9 – Cell Structure and Function (Chapter 3)

11 – Cell Division and the Human Life Cycle (Chapter 17)

13 – **Quiz 1** (Chapters 1 – 3 & 17)– Pattern of Inheritance (Chapter 18)

16 – DNA Biology and Technology (Chapter 19)

18 – **Exam 1** (Chapters 1 – 3 & 17 – 19)

20 – Photosynthesis (Chapter 4)

Personal Activities
1. Track practice Monday and Wednesdays 2 – 4 pm.
2. Track meets on Saturday, October 14th 9 am – 3 pm and Wednesday, Oct. 18th 4 – 7 pm
3. Building with Books fundraiser on Monday, October 9th 5 – 7 pm
4. Photography club meeting on Tuesday October 17th 4 – 5 pm (you are the president)

Sunday	Monday	Tuesday	Wednesday	Thursday	Friday	Saturday
8	9	10	11	12	13	14
15	16	17	18	19	20	21

Independent Reading

Directions: Decide on two books you will read this summer. When reading those books, remain active by noting the following: main ideas, the reasons and details used to support the main ideas, and connections between ideas. Remember to question the validity and cogency of the author's argument, the characters' decisions, and your deductions.

Book 1

Genre	
Title	
Author	
Reason for Choosing Book	

Book 2

Genre	
Title	
Author	
Reason for Choosing Book	

AP Courses

Directions: In order to be considered a competitive candidate when applying for college, students must take AP (Advanced Placement) courses. Go to your high school website and take a look at the AP courses offered. Then go to AP Central (http://apcentral.collegeboard.com/apc/public/courses/teachers_corner/index.html) and take a look at all the AP courses. Choose which APs you are going to take during your high school career. If it is not currently at your school, still write it down and make sure to mention to your principal that you want that course at your school.

Year in High School	AP Courses to Take	
	First Semester	Second Semester
Freshman		
Sophomore		

Junior		
Senior		

www.ingramcontent.com/pod-product-compliance
Lightning Source LLC
LaVergne TN
LVHW081322060426

835509LV00015B/1638